The Window

DEBRA E. WESTMORELAND

Copyright © 2015 Debra E. Westmoreland.

All rights reserved. No part of this book may be used or reproduced by any means, graphic, electronic, or mechanical, including photocopying, recording, taping or by any information storage retrieval system without the written permission of the author except in the case of brief quotations embodied in critical articles and reviews.

Unless otherwise indicated, Scripture taken from the Holy Bible, NEW INTERNATIONAL VERSION®. Copyright © 1973, 1978, 1984 by Biblica, Inc. All rights reserved worldwide. Used by permission. NEW INTERNATIONAL VERSION® and NIV® are registered trademarks of Biblica, Inc. Use of either trademark for the offering of goods or services requires the prior written consent of Biblica US, Inc.

Other scripture quotation is taken from the Amplified Bible, copyright © 1954, 1958, 1962, 1964, 1965, 1987 by The Lockman Foundation. Used by permission.

WestBow Press books may be ordered through booksellers or by contacting:

WestBow Press
A Division of Thomas Nelson & Zondervan
1663 Liberty Drive
Bloomington, IN 47403
www.westbowpress.com
1 (866) 928-1240

Because of the dynamic nature of the Internet, any web addresses or links contained in this book may have changed since publication and may no longer be valid. The views expressed in this work are solely those of the author and do not necessarily reflect the views of the publisher, and the publisher hereby disclaims any responsibility for them.

Any people depicted in stock imagery provided by Thinkstock are models, and such images are being used for illustrative purposes only.
Certain stock imagery © Thinkstock.

ISBN: 978-1-4908-9286-3 (sc)
ISBN: 978-1-4908-9288-7 (hc)
ISBN: 978-1-4908-9287-0 (e)

Library of Congress Control Number: 2015916344

Print information available on the last page.

WestBow Press rev. date: 10/02/2015

CONTENTS

Dedication vii
Acknowledgment ix

1　Be Still and Know That I Am God (Psalm 46:10).. 1
　　DAY 1 1
　　DAY 2 2
　　DAY 3 7
2　Don't Be Afraid, Just Believe (Mark 5:36) 11
　　DAY 4 11
3　The Lord Is My Shepherd (Psalm 23). 25
　　DAY 5 25
　　DAY 6 36
4　For I Know the Plans I Have for You
　　(Jeremiah 29:11). 45
　　DAY 7 45

5	I Will Praise You Forever (Psalm 52:9).	59
	DAY 8	59
	DAY 9	64
	DAY 10	73
6	By Faith (Hebrews 11:1).	79
	DAY 10, Continued	79
	DAY 11	89
7	Those Who Hope in Me Will Not Be Disappointed (Isaiah 49:23).	93
	DAY 12	93
	DAY 13	99

Personal Note from Debra 105
Shared Memories 109

DEDICATION

I dedicate this book to my Lord and Savior for the wonders he has done.

Jeremiah 30:2: "This is what the Lord, the God of Israel, says: Write in a book all the words I have spoken to you."

Psalm 52:9: "I will praise you forever for what you have done; in your name I will hope, for your name is good. I will praise you in the presence of your saints."

ACKNOWLEDGMENT

I would like to thank my good friend, Ray Bush, for drawing the cover for this book. Ray graciously gave his time and talent to be used by God. His artwork has depicted exactly what I envisioned. It is simple, yet speaks powerfully about our intimacy with our God in prayer. As we humbly come into God's presence, we find his strength to help us in our time of need. The warmth of his presence shines into our heart, our lives, and our circumstances. May you feel the warmth of his presence as you read this book.

In the midst of pain, I see your glory.
In the midst of pain, Lord, you are there.
It is your tender, loving mercies that wipe away
these mother's tears.

CHAPTER 1

Be Still and Know That I Am God (Psalm 46:10).

Day 1: The phone rings. If you could know what lies ahead for you from one day to the next, would you really want to? To be honest, I don't think I would. In fact, I probably would fight it kicking and screaming. Yet, as I look back now, the days that we were about to go through have forever changed me. God has forever changed me.

DAY 2: It was a cold winter day—the coldest we'd had in ten years, they said. As I was sitting in the hospital cafeteria, I couldn't help but think, *How did we get here?* Wasn't it less than two weeks ago that we had celebrated Christmas? It had been a joyous time with family and friends, but there was nothing joyous about what was happening now.

Wasn't it yesterday that I spoke with my daughter Stacey? I thought everything was fine, but that wasn't true. As I sat in the hospital cafeteria, my daughter was lying in a hospital bed in the ICU. Nothing can ever prepare a parent for that.

Just yesterday, as I was getting ready for church, I had been listening to one of my favorite preachers on TV. He was talking about God's sustaining grace. I couldn't help but be drawn into everything he was saying. It was like God was saying, "Debra, pay attention. You're going to need to recall every word of this sermon."

It was definitely God's grace that got my family through those thirteen days. It was his grace that paved a way for us, even though I didn't yet understand what he was doing.

Be Still and Know That I Am God (Psalm 46:10).

I can remember the preacher on TV saying it's God's grace, which none of us deserves, that releases his supernatural strength within us when we go through hard times. His grace ignites within us the determination to keep going no matter what.

Prayer: Thank you, God, for your unending grace that you give us daily. It's your grace that sustains us and helps us in our time of need. Even now, as Stacey is in the hospital with a terrible case of what we think is just asthma, your grace is going before us to provide all that she needs. Thank you, Lord.

You would have to know my daughter Stacey. When she graduated from high school, I wrote a letter to her from her dad, George, and me telling her she was our ray of sunshine. From the minute she came into this world, she was always smiling, always laughing, and always talking. I once told her she could carry on a conversation with a wall and it didn't matter that the wall couldn't talk back; she had enough to say for the both of them.

Stacey had asthma since she was a child and was hospitalized several times when she was young, but she never let that get her down. She was a spitfire from the start, and you couldn't tell her that she couldn't do something because then she would go and do it.

I laugh thinking about when she was in kindergarten. I went to her classroom once, and on the wall was what every child wanted to be when they grew up. The list included doctors, nurses, firemen, mommies, and daddies. When I finally found Stacey's artwork, I just laughed. None of those other occupations were good enough for her; my daughter wanted to be a queen. That was our Stacey.

Then there was the time her elementary school had a talent show. As all the parents waited for their little ones to come out and perform, I wondered whether Stacey would truly perform what she had practiced. Sure enough, out came my daughter dancing to MC Hammer. She didn't care what everyone else was doing; she was going to dance her little MC Hammer legs off. Again, that was our Stacey.

Be Still and Know That I Am God (Psalm 46:10).

Her asthma didn't get her down when she was a cheerleader or drill team dancer or when she roller-skated in competitions. She always had a determination to do whatever she wanted and to succeed at whatever she did. I now believe that was a character trait God gave her for times such as this hospitalization. She was going to need that strong will and determination to fight for her life. But we didn't know how tough this fight would be.

I remember when Stacey's dad and I got the phone call from her husband, John David that she was in the hospital. We were concerned, but she had been hospitalized several times when she was a little girl for asthma, and we didn't think this was any different. Yet when I saw her, I quickly realized it was indeed different.

As she lay there trying to appear cheerful, she struggled for every breath she could take. The doctors had put an oxygen mask on her because she was having such difficulty breathing on her own. As I looked into her face, all I could think was this time was definitely different. But I felt God speak to me the words, "Be still and know I am God" (Psalm 46:10).

Prayer: I am still, Lord—more like paralyzed, though. But you alone are God.

As my husband and I went home we thought she would improve by the next day. In situations like this one, you tell yourself everything is going to be fine, but then your mind wanders into those areas of fear and doubt. That was what George and I were feeling.

It's hard to relax and go to sleep when you know your child is in a bad place. I can understand now what parents go through when they sit by their child's bedside feeling helpless and afraid. Yet looking back, God would not let me stay in that place for long. Each time I felt myself slipping down the path of fear and doubt, God was there with a verse or a word from a dear friend to reassure us he had the situation under his control.

We had so many precious friends and family members praying for Stacey and our family. I truly don't see how people can get through hard times without God on their side. But the days ahead were going to test our faith.

DAY 3: I got up early that morning, wanting to get to the hospital as soon as visiting hours began in the ICU. I couldn't wait to see Stacey's face. I just wanted a glimpse of her feeling a little better, but when I got there, she wasn't. Stacey tried to smile, but I knew she was scared too.

They had put a full-face mask on her because she needed more oxygen. I could see her chest moving up and down with such force as she seemed to struggle harder for every breath she could get. The doctors were testing her for everything, including pneumonia and even swine flu. Her chest X-rays showed her condition was getting worse.

I didn't want to leave her bedside. When I did have to leave because of medicine changes or nurses attending to her needs, I would pace the hallway. There was a window at the end of the hallway where I could feel the warmth of the sun's rays coming through. I gravitated toward its bright rays, as if God was beckoning me to come into his presence.

Again I could hear him say, "Debra, be still and know I am God.

Prayer: Okay, Lord, I know you're God. Help me; come quickly to help my daughter.

There's not a lot to do in a hospital when you have to leave your loved one's room. The ICU had certain visiting hours, and the nurses were just wonderful to let our family stay longer than we were allowed. One time the nurses came in to do some medicine changes and said I needed to leave, but my response was, "I'm not going anywhere!" I don't remember saying that, but a nurse later told me they knew not to mess with a concerned mama.

As I walked the hospital halls between visiting hours, I saw a lot of concerned mothers. A Bible study I participated in helped to occupy my mind and keep me in God's Word calming my fears.

One day while I was in the cafeteria waiting to go back to ICU, I turned to Malachi as I opened my Bible to work on my Bible study lesson. That's part of the Bible I don't normally turn to, yet I felt God pointing me to Malachi 4:2, which reads, "But for you who revere my name, the sun of righteousness

Be Still and Know That I Am God (Psalm 46:10).

will rise with healing in its wings. And you will go out and leap like calves released from the stall."

I knew this was a promise from God. I told the Lord, "I don't feel like leaping for joy right now, but I'll trust you. I'll wait on you to rise with healing in your wings for my precious Stacey."

Prayer: Dear Lord, your Word is truth. Help me to hang on to every word you give me. Your Word is what I cling to right now.

CHAPTER 2

Don't Be Afraid, Just Believe (Mark 5:36).

DAY 4: I was now in a routine: get up early, get dressed, and go out the door with my hospital bag in tow. In it I had all I needed for another long day at the hospital—my Bible along with my lesson plus a water bottle and snacks.

I drove to the hospital wondering how Stacey had done through the night, and then my doubts and fears started to creep back in. The Enemy knows just how to attack to get our focus off God.

I started thinking that my husband and I would never see our daughter start a family. Stacey and her precious husband had been married for three years, and they had been talking about having children soon. Her husband, John David, wanted a big family, but Stacey would have been happy with just one or two children.

John David was a wonderful son-in-law, and he was truly an answer to our prayers for her as a husband. I remember praying for God to bring a godly man into Stacey's life right after she had a terrible breakup with a young man her dad and I did not approve of. Before that relationship was officially over, Stacey called me wanting me and her dad to reconsider our feelings about this young man. I thought she was over him, yet he was secretly trying to win her back.

God had given me a verse during my quiet time with him one morning as I was praying over this relationship. He said in Titus 2:12, "It teaches us to say no to ungodliness and worldly passions, and to live self-controlled, upright and godly lives." I knew God was saying, "This is not the young man I have for her, and you must stand firm." I did the hardest thing I had ever done with my daughter, which was to oppose her wishes and stand firm in my beliefs. I told her if she ever wanted our blessings, she would have to break it off completely with this man. I am so thankful she did, and God opened the way for her to meet the man of her dreams.

As I walked into the ICU, her doctor was there for his morning rounds. This was another reason I wanted to get there right when they allowed visitors; you could catch the doctors as they went from room to room. I always had lots of questions for him, and I am sure he hated to see me coming.

He wanted to give us good news, but on this day it was not what I wanted to hear. Her x-rays were again getting worse, and her breathing was not getting any better either. He mentioned a word I was not prepared to hear: *ventilator*! That word scared me to death. You always hear about people who have to go on a ventilator and never come off. Stacey was scared too. I think she knew now that she was in big trouble. The doctor said it would help

The Window

with her breathing. Her body needed to rest and have a chance to fight whatever was attacking her.

Her doctor still had no clue what it was. He had to label her with something, so they called it asthma and pneumonia. But there was a person in ICU who indeed did have H1N1, and he still felt that was a possibility even though her tests had come back negative. He put her on every medicine he could think of just in case it was.

I remember the nurses coming in with the doctor to tell Stacey she needed to be put on a ventilator. She was so upset. Then she had to sign a bunch of papers allowing them to do this and going over all the things that could happen. Then to make it worse, the chaplain came in to talk to her, discussing things she didn't want to talk about. The nurses could see the concerned look on our faces, and they were quick to assure us there would be no problems. I know they say that to all their patients, but I wanted to know there would indeed be no problems!

I hated leaving the room as they prepared to hook her up to the ventilator. I gave her a hug and kiss then left the room. Again I paced up and down that hall, repeating every verse God had given us so far. One verse that my leader, Lynn, in my Bible study gave me was Isaiah 26:3, "You will keep in perfect peace him whose mind is steadfast, because he trusts in you." I must have repeated that verse a million times as I paced up and down that hallway.

The window at the end of the hallway was again drawing me with its rays of light shining through (remember Malachi 4:2). There I felt peace and God's comfort, and I waited for the Sun of righteousness to rise with healing in its wings. His words to me that day were in Mark 5:36: "Don't be afraid, just believe."

Prayer: Lord, I am afraid. Help me to not be afraid and just believe you to be who you say you are.

Nothing prepares you for what you will see as your loved one is hooked up to a machine that is doing the breathing for her. I remember going in to see her for the first time. There were so many wires going everywhere, but what I saw was that my daughter was at peace. I felt a sense of relief; no longer was she struggling for every breath. She was also put into an induced coma so her body would not fight the ventilator. I again heard God's words: "Debra, don't be afraid. Just believe."

You know fear comes easy for a mother. I think the minute your children are born and you look into their little faces, you think of all the different scenarios of their little lives. Will they be healthy? Will they do well in school? Will they succeed in life? Will they get married and have children? Then even more fear sets in—now there are grandchildren. *Worry, worry, worry!*

Let me first start with Stacey's health. She had a rough time even before she was born. I had high blood pressure from the beginning of my pregnancy with her. I ended up being under complete bed rest beginning my eighth month of pregnancy, and to complicate matters, I developed toxemia. She wasn't even born yet, and she was giving us problems. Then after she was born, we could tell she was going to have allergies, which she inherited from me. She also developed asthma, and again she inherited it from yours truly.

Then there was the time when she was eighteen months old. She was starting to really enjoy solid food, so one day I made her a peanut butter and jelly sandwich—big mistake. She smeared peanut butter all over her little face and ate not even a bite, and we noticed her face starting to swell and wheezing in her chest. Well after a trip to the emergency room, we found out that she was indeed allergic to peanut butter, which would begin a lifelong fear of checking everything she put in her mouth.

Thank the Lord for EpiPens, which she has only had to use once when she ate a cookie in high school that contained nuts. I was at Bible study, and apparently she had tried to call me asking permission to use the EpiPen on herself. Can you imagine? Her throat was closing up, and she wanted her mama to tell her to inject herself with a medication to save her life. Thank the Lord she chose to go ahead and use it.

Now let's talk about her school years. Stacey always had a difficult time in school. She always struggled with reading and comprehension. During her third-grade year, her teacher urged us to have her tested at Children's Scottish Rites Hospital for learning problems. She indeed showed signs of a learning disability, which they labeled as short-term memory loss. She had trouble with comprehension and recall of what she had learned.

I would see her get frustrated with reading and taking tests so many times. We tried everything to help her. I would even record some chapters in her books and have her listen as she read along. Stacey never gave up, but secretly I knew she was hurting. And it didn't help when friends would brag about all their good grades, knowing Stacey was struggling just to make Cs, and then they had the nerve to ask to see her report card to make her feel even worse. You know, sometimes kids can be so cruel, and as a mama you just want to smack them. What Stacey lacked in grades in school, she made up for with an outgoing personality.

Stacey did cheerleading and drill team in grade school, and every Saturday we would go to the football games and see her perform. Stacey could not do a cartwheel or jump up high like the other

Don't Be Afraid, Just Believe (Mark 5:36).

girls, but she had a voice on her that could outscream her teammates.

She later decided to roller skate. We took her once to a birthday party, and she couldn't even begin to stand up on skates, much less actually roller skate. Why we ever signed her up for skating lessons I don't know. I believe God had a hand in this because he knew it would be good for her to build her self-confidence and self-esteem. Her skating coaches didn't at first think she would ever pass from one level to the next. She did not like her feet to come off the ground, and they had to for her to pass. However, she passed every level. This turned into years of skating lessons, and she eventually went on to compete in skating competitions. She even earned medals in her figure skating and dance competitions. It wasn't, however, her receiving medals that was important to us. It was seeing her proud of every accomplishment she made. But this too had its challenges; her coach, Bubba, whom she loved, suddenly died. We wondered if she would want to continue with her skating after losing someone she became so close to, but she did and we were glad.

Then God gave her a very godly man for a skating coach. His name was Mr. Ralph. Mr. Ralph was like a grandfather to Stacey. One thing I will always remember about Mr. Ralph was no matter how he was doing, he would always say, "If I was any better, I couldn't stand myself." He was a very positive person, and that was exactly what Stacey needed. Mr. Ralph was also a great encourager and knew how to challenge Stacey to go beyond her comfort zone. As she was preparing for nationals, she found out she needed to learn to skate on in-line skates. Mr. Ralph felt like she could do it and stand a better chance at getting a medal since this was considered new to the sport.

The first time she put on in-line skates, it looked like a toddler trying to learn how to walk. Stacey was determined to master these skates, and she did. She and Mr. Ralph picked out a country and western song called "Little Bitty" to dance to at nationals, and this just fit her perfectly. Her costume was a blue jacket and skirt with rhinestones all over it. She

Don't Be Afraid, Just Believe (Mark 5:36).

even had rhinestones on her blue suede cowgirl hat and made-up cowgirl boots.

When the day for nationals came, we headed for Fresno, California. This was truly the big leagues, and her dad and I were so nervous. But Stacey was in her element and just shined as she performed to her song. When they called her name to the podium and gave her third place, our eyes filled with tears as she accepted her medal. I don't know who was more proud—us or her coach. Shortly thereafter, this coach, whom she had come to love dearly, died also. I think she lost her passion for skating after that and only continued for another year.

When she graduated high school, she wanted to be a hair stylist. This fit her personality. We knew college would be hard for her and thought this would be a career she could do well in. After all, she had the personality for it. She loved to talk, which we already knew, and people seemed to love to talk back to her. She was also able to get a thousand-dollar scholarship to a well-known beauty school.

I remember the first six weeks were the hardest because she had to learn the fundamentals of cutting hair. All she wanted to do was pick up a pair of scissors and start creating a Stacey masterpiece. I laughed the first time she cut my hair. She needed a model for class, and of course, her mama was going to help out. Little did I know after I got up out of that chair and looked in the mirror my bangs were cut to the top of my forehead. Oh well, it was just hair, and hair would grow. She quickly caught on and graduated with flying colors. Next was the test to pass her state board exam. Did I mention the word *worry* enough! We will pick up from there later.

 As I saw Stacey lying in that bed in a coma, I was glad she couldn't see her hair. Stacey had auburn-colored hair, which was just beautiful. Of course after being in beauty school it had become just about every color in the rainbow. The nurses had to pull her hair up into a little ball on top of her head so her hair would be out of the way from all the tubes and wires that seemed to go everywhere. After a while you become glued to all the wires and monitors that showed her heart rate, blood pressure, oxygen levels, etc.

Don't Be Afraid, Just Believe (Mark 5:36).

Every time her heart rate would go up, I would panic. Sometimes I felt her blood pressure would cause her to have a stroke because it would go up so high. The nurses would always reassure us she was okay, but I know they weren't telling us what they really knew and felt. I wondered if Stacey felt scared and that was making her blood pressure soar. Then to complicate matters, blood started to appear in her urine. I had watched enough TV medical shows to know this was not a good sign. They had to call in an urologist. He wanted to run tests to see where the source of the blood was coming from. Again they try to reassure you that it is just an irritation of the catheter. I was not buying it. Were they concerned that her kidneys were failing because of all the stress her body was under? That was certainly where my mind was going.

Prayer: Lord, calm my fears. You tell me not to be afraid, but I am.

CHAPTER 3

The Lord Is My Shepherd (Psalm 23).

Day 5: As I walked into Stacey's room that morning, there sat my Bible study leader, Lynn. She lived close to the hospital, and her presence seemed to always calm me. I walked over to Stacey's bedside and just rubbed her feet. She loved a good foot massage. I did that a lot, putting lotion on her legs and on her feet. I felt this was one way I could help my daughter. I was thankful Lynn was there when the doctor came by. He again did not have good news. Stacey's infection—whatever it was—was getting worse. He wanted to extract fluid from Stacey's lungs and then test it to see what it was to possibly know how to treat it. He wanted to do the procedure as soon as possible. I wondered if he thought Stacey was running out of time. The problem, however, was that the equipment needed to perform the procedure would not be available until the afternoon.

As Lynn and I stepped out of Stacey's room, we went to the end of the hallway next to the window I was coming to love and started praying. No matter what this looked like, we were going to pray and trust God with the outcome. And as soon as we finished praying, Stacey's doctor came over and said that all of a sudden the equipment he needed had become available for the procedure. He looked so surprised, but Lynn and I knew this was indeed God. How we praised him in that hallway. It didn't seem to take that long for them to do the procedure, but now all we could do was wait.

I was never good at waiting. If we are honest, none of us are. Waiting causes us to trust God with

The Lord Is My Shepherd (Psalm 23).

the outcome we don't have any control over. As I waited God had a way of bringing back to my mind all the times I was in his waiting room, waiting for him to answer my prayers, waiting for him to come through in a situation. He reminded me of his faithfulness to me in each waiting room situation.

I recalled waiting for Stacey's test results from her cosmetology test. This was so hard for her. We knew the test would be a challenge. She knew she had mastered the hands-on part of the test. But then there was the written part of the test. We thought we had a plan that would at least help in that situation. Her good friend Allegra came with us; she was such an encourager to Stacey. Allegra was going to college and majoring in English, and we planned for her to go with Stacey to help read her the test questions. Yet we quickly found out that they would not allow it. Their response was, "If she fails, she can just take it over and over and over." Obviously there was not a lot of compassion when it came to taking a state board test.

So Stacey took the written test, and as she came out of the building, I could tell she was concerned.

We went home, and what else, we waited. George and I were out of town when Stacey got the letter from Austin, and when she opened the envelope, she had indeed failed. Oh, how my heart ached for her. She would have to retake it again in a few months. Those months went by slowly as she waited and studied and prepared to retake the test. Her sweet friend Allegra would take her study books and read them on tape for Stacey to listen and follow along with. She would read her questions and have Stacey answer them. She was such a blessing to us and Stacey. I knew God was telling us and Stacey that she could do this test on her own and he was going to be the one that would bring her the victory.

As we prepared to go back to Austin, the Lord gave me such peace about this test. God again reminded me of his faithfulness to Stacey when she went away to a camp in high school. This was the first time she had ever been away from us. All I could do was worry about her asthma and allergies out in the middle of the woods with every possible pollen attacking my precious daughter. It is amazing how our minds wander into scenarios that never take place. I am so good at that, and God knows I have a vivid imagination. God gave me Psalm 112:7–8: "He will have no fear of bad news; his heart is steadfast, trusting in the Lord. His heart is secure, he will have no fear; in the end he will look in triumph on his foes." I claimed that verse for her at camp, and she came home with no health problems and had a great time. I claimed that verse again as she prepared to retake her cosmetology test.

We got up early that morning and drove back to Austin. Before Stacey went in to retake her test, we prayed as a family that God would give her victory. Then she bravely went into the building on her own and retook her test. Again, George and I sat and waited anxiously for her to finish. After what seemed like an eternity, we began to see people come out of the building. We noticed that some looked confident while others looked like Stacey after the first time she took her test: scared, bewildered, and discouraged. I began to repeat that verse in Psalms, and then I saw Stacey exit the building. I looked at her face, and I could tell she was more confident.

We praised God for being with her and helping her finish on her own. Then we waited for the results.

The day Stacey got her letter in the mail, I was in the kitchen putting up dishes I had washed. She brought the letter over to me. We were both so nervous as she opened it. I think we prayed first, and then she opened the envelope. All she saw was that she had passed! We were so excited that we just jumped for joy. Remember, jumping was something that Stacey didn't normally do, but we jumped and praised God.

Now as I was waiting for these tests to come back from this procedure on Stacey's lungs, God again reminded me of those verses in Psalm 112. A good friend named Joanne from my Bible study had these verses in her devotional and wanted to share them with me. But what was so funny was she did not want to give me the first part of the verses. She just repeated the last part that says, "His heart is secure, he will have no fear; in the end he will look in triumph on his foes." I told her, "Joanne, you did not repeat the whole verse. The best part is in that first verse that says, 'He will have no fear of bad

The Lord Is My Shepherd (Psalm 23).

news.'" That was what I was claiming as I paced up and down that hallway outside of Stacey's room. Again the window at the end of the hallway called me to come and bathe in the sun's rays. I again felt the presence of God, and he gave me his peace.

Prayer: Lord, help me to remain steadfast and not be afraid. I will trust in you to bring Stacey the victory of complete healing. She will triumph over her foes.

The day seemed to drag on as we waited. Some friends of Stacey and John David came to visit; we circled around Stacey's bed and prayed over her. I wondered if Stacey could sense our presence as we prayed. She looked so peaceful, but I knew her body was wearing out. Her urine continued to show signs of blood, and now there appeared to be a fever. George came after work; I was so glad he was staying in town. He would work all day and come up to the hospital at night, where we would stay until they kicked us out. Then Stacey's precious husband would come in and stay with her. He was trying to work and fighting his own battle with what we thought was just a cold or bronchitis, but in reality we found out he also had pneumonia. He would try to work and then go home for breathing treatments and then come to the hospital to be with Stacey.

We finally talked John David into going to the doctor to get on antibiotics. The hospital would make him wear a mask around Stacey so as not to infect her with any germs. John David was so precious with how he lovingly helped to take care of his wife. He would often help the nurses give Stacey a sponge bath. He would even help wash and comb her hair. Oh, how I was glad Stacey couldn't see her hair. There are advantages to being so sedated that you can't know how you look and what is going on. But did she really know? John David would often stay way beyond visiting hours. After we went home for the night, the nurses in ICU would let him stay. They were so kind and compassionate to our needs. We were truly blessed to have such a wonderful son-in-law and wonderful nurses who went above and beyond what they had to do. God was so good!

Well the time had come; our waiting was over. I remember as we came down the hall to Stacey's room, there sat her doctor on the computer going over the test results. Then the words came out of his mouth that I did not expect. He said, "This is really kicking my butt."

Now that is not what you want to hear from your doctor. But you could tell he was really frustrated. The tests did not really give any indication as to what was attacking Stacey. He stated that the results were fifty/fifty, which meant there was 50 percent chance it could be bacterial and a 50 percent chance it could be viral. So again he labeled it severe asthma and pneumonia, and the H1N1 was still negative. He immediately thought it was best to bring on an infectious disease doctor. This doctor reviewed all of Stacey's x-rays and test results and then put Stacey on a different round of antibiotics and other medicines. Stacey was also taking high doses of steroids; I think they were bringing out all the big guns they could possibly think of.

I could feel myself slipping into that scary place that none of us want to go to. Was I indeed going to lose my daughter? Did I misunderstand God? No, I would not let myself go there. I kept claiming every verse God put in front of me.

It was during this time that I was studying Psalm 23 in my Bible study. This was not exactly my most favorite Psalm. After all, this was the Psalm everyone repeated when someone was dying or would use at their funeral. But God was helping me see this Psalm in a different way, which gave me peace and renewed my trust in him.

Psalm 23 starts out with, "The Lord is my Shepherd." The Bible often refers to our Lord as a Shepherd and a good one at that. A shepherd knows his sheep and has an intimate relationship with each one. A shepherd's job is a tireless one, often going without sleep as he is on duty constantly. He will lead the way for his sheep and smooth the rough places as well as gently help his sheep over dangerous places. He is also on guard for false shepherds that would try to come and attack or steal his beloved sheep. But his sheep know their shepherd's voice and will not follow another; they will even run from another's voice. A shepherd also has a staff or rod that he uses to gently guide his sheep and as a weapon in case of danger.

As I studied this Psalm, I began see it as a source of comfort that gave me peace as I viewed the Lord as my daughter's Good Shepherd. I wrote in my journal that night, "The Lord is Stacey's shepherd. She is in a place where all her needs are being met. The Lord has made her to lie down in green pastures—green with nourishment from all her IV fluids, medications, and feeding tubes. He is restoring her soul and guiding her in paths of righteousness for his name's sake. Even though she is walking through some scary and tough times, she will fear no evil. For you, God, are with her, and your rod and your staff give her comfort. You will and have prepared a table for her filled with every weapon of medicine that you have given her doctors in the presence of whatever enemy that is attacking her body. You anoint her head with oil, and her cup overflows. Surely goodness and your love will follow her all the days of her *long* life, and she will dwell in the house of the Lord forever."

Day 6: By now the days were running together. We had our routine and even had our certain places in the hospital where we would go and sit in between visiting hours. Friends from our church would come and visit with us and pray with us. They were such a source of support and comfort. We were careful, though, not to invite many visitors. For one thing, I did not want to leave Stacey's room to see people who had come by. I was always afraid that if I left her bedside, something might happen. I know our family and dear friends wanted to be there for us, but I was afraid that if they saw the seriousness of Stacey in how she looked, I would see their fear and immediately crumble into a puddle of tears.

I think this was also God's way of protecting us. He had us so closely wrapped in his arms as our Good Shepherd, and there was not going to be any influence from the Evil One that would discourage us. It was hard to tell those I was closest to that they should just pray, and I would update them as often as I could.

There was, however, a sweet friend of Stacey's who was there often during those critical days. Her name was Marissa. She was a godsend to us.

The Lord Is My Shepherd (Psalm 23).

She would often just show up when we were in the hospital cafeteria. Her presence also gave me such peace. She was always there to lend a helping hand, to get us coffee or just put her arm around us. I laugh at the time when she wanted to help me with all my stuff I brought with me wherever I went. She would not let me carry anything. She just picked up all my bags and led the way for us to go back to Stacey's room. There was one time, though, as she left I caught her wiping her eyes as if she was crying. I knew she was holding it together for us, but she was scared like we were for her precious friend.

Stacey had now been on the ventilator for several days, and they wanted to try and see if they could back off on the oxygen in hopes that she could breathe more on her own. It did not go well, though. As they tried to back off, she immediately started coughing with such force that I thought her whole body was going to go into convulsions. They decided she was not ready, and she needed the machine to do the breathing for her. Then her chest x-rays came back with no change, but at least they were no worse.

The Window

The nurses seemed to me to be quieter than usual. They came in often to check all her vitals and make medicine changes, but I wondered what they were really thinking. You know things are not going well when the nurses don't have anything encouraging to say. They asked me to step out into the hallway as they changed Stacey's bedding and to reposition her. I reluctantly got up, and I again paced up and down that hallway. I must have walked miles in the hallway. My mind was racing with what we were up against, and it seemed the Enemy was winning.

But then God knows just what to do to get our minds off of ourselves. He had Lynn show up at just the right time. I think she could see I was beginning to get weary. She walked with me down to the end of the hallway next to the window where I would often feel God's presence. There the sun's rays came shining through the window and enveloped us. Then Lynn did exactly what I needed her to do: she put her arms around me, and we prayed. But it wasn't her arms I felt; it was the arms of my Lord and Savior who had me close in his embrace. In that moment I did something I had not totally

The Lord Is My Shepherd (Psalm 23).

done before. I totally surrendered my daughter to my Lord. I placed her at the feet of Jesus and said, "Lord, in health I will praise you and in sickness I will praise you; whatever your will, I will praise you." Notice I didn't say death. I just couldn't say the words, yet the Lord knew my heart, and he knew I was letting go of my will and accepting whatever his will was.

After we prayed, I felt like a weight had been lifted off of my shoulders. Though I had trusted God to help us, I had not totally surrendered Stacey into his hands for whatever his will and plan was for her. As Lynn left I returned to Stacey's room; there was no change. I would work on my Bible study, step out for a bite to eat, and return to again sit by her bedside. Then again the nurses would come in to do their thing, and I would have to return to the hallway, where I would do what I was good at: pace up and down.

There in the hallway I heard, "Code blue, code blue," go out over the intercom. It was not to Stacey's room that the nurses ran but to another room where a patient was in distress. I felt relieved that it was not Stacey to whom they were running to save but to another. This made me feel guilty though. Could that mother of that loved one be pacing up and down that hallway just like me praying for God to save her child? Then the Enemy did what he is so good at. The thought came to mind, *Stacey will be next.* Again God reminded me of what I had prayed, and Stacey was his, no matter what.

As I was pacing, I happened to pass a computer at one of the nurses' stations, and on it was a picture of a couple holding their baby with a friend next to the mother. This picture drew me closer. It was as if God was saying, "Debra, come closer to what I want to show you." So I studied the picture again, and what I saw brought me to tears. It was a picture of a mother with her child in what looked like a hospital bed. She had short auburn hair, cut just like Stacey; she even looked like Stacey. Then there was a man next to her who had to be her husband. He had a baseball cap on and looked just like John David, who always wore a ball cap. Then there appeared to be a friend next to the mother who resembled Stacey's precious friend Marissa. I just stared at the picture for what seemed like an eternity. I could feel God say, "Debra, study this picture, for what I have showed you will come to pass. You will see your daughter with her child. Just believe."

That evening when we left Stacey's room to go home, there was no change. I remember always asking George, "Do you think Stacey is going to be all right?" My precious husband always said what I needed him to say: "Yes, it is going to just take time. We have to trust God." He was always so strong, yet I knew he had his moments as well. He would put up a good front for me, but I know he was just as scared. God was also drawing George to a closer walk with himself through this journey with our daughter. We would share with each other devotional passages that God was speaking to each of us. How I treasured those moments, and they gave us both such strength. I know God was bringing so much good out of this crisis with Stacey.

That night as we went to bed, I had a dream. Remember me saying that I had been studying Psalm 23 in my Bible study. Jesus kept reminding me that he was our Good Shepherd who watches over his sheep. Well that night in my dream, that sheep pen had an invader that was up to no good. He had invaded our home, not by the front door but through the window next to my rocking chair in the living room. In the hallway I could hear voices. One voice was familiar and the other was not. Then I could see a dark outline of someone (the Enemy) lurking just outside of our bedroom door. There was also a bright light illuminating from somewhere just behind the intruder. I could hear their voices as if they were in a discussion over something.

George and I were in bed, but we could not move. It was as if we were paralyzed, unable to move, just like Stacey. Then all of a sudden the Enemy left. He left by the same way he had come in, which was through the window.

The next morning I kept thinking about this dream and what, if anything, it meant. The Lord then spoke to me, saying: "Debra, don't you understand? The intruder was Satan. He entered your home in deception to bring harm to your family."

This is what we had studied in my Bible study lesson. The enemy, false shepherd never enters by the gate but always by another means, so as to not be detected. The Lord then went on to explain to me that our bedroom represented the sheep pen that held our family. We were paralyzed and helpless to defend ourselves like Stacey. The dark figure I saw outside our bedroom was the Enemy, and the light I saw illuminating the hallway was Jesus himself. They were in a conversation, and Jesus was telling Satan he had no power here. He was not going to penetrate his sheep pen, and he commanded him to leave by the same way he came in. It was then that I understood that Jesus was reassuring me that the Enemy did try to attack my family, namely my daughter, but he had no power to do so. Just like John 10:10 says, "The thief comes only to steal and kill and destroy; I have come that they may have life, and have it to the full."

Prayer: Thank you Lord, you are our Good Shepherd and the Enemy has no power over you. You will defend your sheep pen. In you there is life and life abundantly.

CHAPTER 4

For I Know the Plans I Have for You (Jeremiah 29:11).

DAY 7: It was the weekend, and George and I were up early, anxious to get back to the hospital. As I was getting ready, my mind started to reminisce over past sweet memories of our daughter. In my hallway I have lots of family pictures that are dear to me. There are pictures of Stacey when she was a baby, pictures of when she was in skating, and pictures of her and John David's wedding day. In every picture she always had the biggest smile; oh how I would love to see that smile one more time. I knew George felt the same way too; we both just wanted our Stacey back.

Stacey was such a Daddy's girl. She had him wrapped around her little finger, and he loved it. I remember when Stacey was born, the minute she came into this world her daddy's heart just melted for his precious daughter. It was so funny when the nurses took Stacey down to the nursery to put her name tag on her, who do you think followed? That is right, it was George. He didn't stay behind to be with his wife; oh no, he had to make sure they put the right name tag on his little girl.

Stacey looked so much like her daddy that there would be no denying whose child she was. Stacey and George always had a special bond that only little girls and their daddies have. They would have a standing date every Saturday morning at Waffle House to eat breakfast, and then George would take Stacey to her skating lessons at the skating rink. This was their routine for years, and do you think I

For I Know the Plans I Have for You (Jeremiah 29:11).

was ever invited? No, but I loved that this was their special time together.

Then came the day when Stacey and John David were to be married. This was a fairy tale wedding. It was a fairly big wedding too, with over three hundred guests. I was a little concerned that George wasn't going to be able to keep it together to walk his little girl down the aisle, but he did. I was so proud of him; he squeezed my hand when he sat down after giving her hand in marriage to John David. I thought I saw tears streaming down his face, but I couldn't look or else we both would have been sobbing, and Stacey would have probably killed us both right there.

Another special memory was at the wedding reception. We held it at a big hotel filled with family and friends. It was truly a magical night, with Stacey just beaming and smiling in her bridal gown. Then came the moment for the father/daughter dance. Stacey had picked out the song "Butterfly Kisses," which was always the song she wanted played at her wedding for her and her daddy to dance to. As they both met together on the dance floor, my heart was bursting with pride for this special man and his beloved daughter. As soon as they started to dance, both of them started to cry. There they danced and danced, with streams of tears running down both of their faces. I don't think there was a dry eye in the ballroom that night.

That night seemed so long ago as I stared at those pictures. Sometimes, though, it helped to look back at special moments to help you cope with what was going on in the present. Well, little did we know that today God was going to show us that those who trust in him will not be disappointed. Little did we know that soon we would see that smile once again on our precious daughter's face.

When we walked into the ICU, we saw Stacey's doctor. They had taken Stacey to get a chest x-ray, which they had done every day, but today her doctor said there was a slight improvement. Her lungs actually looked a little less cloudy, which meant that the new medicines were working; God was working. In that moment I could have hugged him; he actually looked like he needed a hug. This was the first time he had anything good to tell us.

For I Know the Plans I Have for You (Jeremiah 29:11).

He wanted to try again to get Stacey to the point where they would back her off the ventilator. He wanted to reduce the amount of oxygen she was getting from the machine in hopes of her breathing more and more on her own. This made me so nervous. After all, she did not do well the first time they had tried. But they needed to see how she would respond, and I think he also thought this would give him a good indication of how she was improving. This was going to be a slow process and would also be a long couple of days.

As they prepared to slowly start the process of backing her off the ventilator, I started praying that one verse that I prayed over Stacey every day: "You will keep in perfect peace, he whose mind is steadfast because he trusts in you." Stacey needed to remain calm with good blood pressure and heart rate. I think the nurses were a little anxious as they started the process, but God was true to his word. Stacey was calm, with good blood pressure and heart rate. She did start to cough at first, but shortly she quieted down and began breathing a little more on her own.

The Window

It is funny how we see God working on our behalf and see him answering our prayers, and we stand in awe of what he is doing. Whenever I stepped out of her room, I would again pace the hallway as I had done for so many days, but this time I was praising his name for what he had done. As I bathed in his presence by the window with his sunbeams coming through, I felt him say: "Debra, remember my words to you in Malachi 4:2: 'But for you who revere my name, the sun of righteousness will rise with healing in its wings. And you will go out and leap like calves released from the stall.' Rise and see my healing is coming to your daughter."

Oh, how I praised him next to that window. I phoned friends and loved ones to give them good news for once and to thank them for all their prayers for my daughter. Joanne stopped by with a verse for me in 1 Peter 1:6–7, "In this you greatly rejoice though now for a little while you may have had to suffer grief in all kinds of trials. These have come so that your faith of greater worth than gold, which perishes even though refined by fire—may be proved genuine and may result in praise, glory and honor when Jesus Christ is revealed." This verse did indeed fit everything that we had endured over these past several days with our daughter.

As I watched my daughter, I couldn't help but wipe away tears. Every tear the Lord counted, measured, and carried close to his heart, knowing how we were at times just hanging on to every word of Scripture he had given us. And now after many tears that had been shed, it was time to rejoice and give all praise to my heavenly Father.

This was the first time I actually felt the word *hope*, a word that means different things to different people. Some would describe hope as wishful thinking. People say the word often when they don't know what else to say. "I have hope that everything will turn out okay," yet in our hearts we secretly wonder if it will. Real hope is what sustains us as we learn to patiently wait for God to fulfill what we believe he has promised us.

I like the verse in Hebrews 11:1 that says, "Now faith is being sure of what we hope for and certain of what we do not see." God was giving us his hope as we waited for him to fulfill what we believed he had promised us in his Word.

The first time I really understood that verse was when we were praying for what to do when Stacey finished elementary school and was about to start middle school. We really did not want to put her in the middle school near our house. It was such a big school, and we didn't think Stacey would receive the needed help with her studies. I started to pray as to what we should do.

One Sunday our youth pastor gave the sermon on Jeremiah 29:11, "For I know the plans I have for you, declares the Lord, plans to prosper you and not to harm you, plans to give you hope and a future." I had never heard of that verse, and it just grabbed me. That was exactly what we were praying for our daughter, a hope and a future. To hear that God had a perfect plan for us and that each plan was individual to meet the needs for each specific person was what I needed to hear.

After that sermon, I committed this verse to prayer, trusting God to lead us in the right way. Then came an opportunity for us to meet with a

For I Know the Plans I Have for You (Jeremiah 29:11).

principal at a private school that was on the campus of Dallas Baptist University. It was their lab school with kindergarten through seventh grade. I had heard such wonderful things about this school and felt with the small class size that each grade had, this would be a great environment for Stacey to learn in.

As I sat in the office waiting for a meeting with the principal, I wondered if she would be receptive to Stacey's special needs and learning difficulties. It seemed like I was in that waiting room (don't you love how God has a way of just making us wait and wait and wait, yet if he gave us everything when we wanted it, we would never trust him; he is so smart) for what seemed like hours. As I sat there quietly praying for God's control over this meeting, I looked down and saw a pamphlet about the university on a small coffee table. I picked it up and started reading about the university and all it had to offer to their students. Then I felt the Holy Spirit say, "Turn the pamphlet over." When I did, there staring at me was the university's scripture verse that they claimed. Guess what that verse was? Jeremiah 29:11. How good of God to show me this was his confirmation of where he wanted Stacey to be.

When I finally met the principal, she was very gracious but concerned that the school could not meet Stacey's special academic needs. I tried my best to reassure her that Stacey was a hard worker and we would do our part to help and support her with all her studies. But all she said was that she would have to pray about it. Well I left there a little disappointed, but I believed God would work it out if he truly wanted her there.

It seemed like days went by before we finally received a call from the principal. She proceeded to tell me that she had her mind made up that this was not going to be a good fit for our daughter, yet she felt God was telling her this was his plan for Stacey to attend this school. I was so glad that she had listened to her heart and not her head. Stacey attended that school for two years and received excellent, godly teaching from teachers who took a special interest in her. They even helped tutor her after school on their own time to help her excel in her class work. In those two years, Stacey grew

For I Know the Plans I Have for You (Jeremiah 29:11).

in her self-confidence and began to dream big for what her future would hold. Indeed, God had a great future filled with hope for our daughter, and nothing was going to stand in his way to fulfill what he had planned.

This day seemed to drag on, but with each passing hour, I felt that my daughter was returning to us. They also started to reduce the amount of medication they had been giving her to keep her in a somewhat coma state. I could tell that she was starting to be aware of things around her. She would start to move her legs and arms. She seemed the most irritated when she moved her hands, which she could not easily do since they had her in restraints. This was a precaution in case she tried to pull out every tube she had going into her body, and there were tubes going everywhere. They were wise in keeping her in restraints, because knowing Stacey, she would indeed have pulled out everything she could get her hands on.

It was starting to get late in the afternoon, and I noticed that she was starting to move her head back and forth. Her little eyes were starting to open ever so slightly. Now she was getting agitated with the restraints. It was as if she had no clue where she was or what was going on. We tried to calm her down, telling her where she was and what was going on.

About that time her husband, John David, came in. She got excited because I know she could hear his voice. She started taking her right hand and pounding it on the bed. She was actually trying to form words in her mouth, but it was very hard to understand her with a tube in her throat. John David finally understood that she wanted to write. So we got some paper and a pen and placed it on the bed next to her hand. Every time we placed the pen in her hand, though, she would drop it. She had so little strength that it was difficult to hold on to it long enough to form a word.

She would not give up; she was bound and determined to let us know what she had to say. Finally she would move the pen across the paper, forming letters that we would try to decipher. I felt like we were on a game show, "Guess that Word." After many attempts we figured out that she was forming the letter C. We would say the letter and

For I Know the Plans I Have for You (Jeremiah 29:11).

she would shake her head as if to say yes. Okay, one letter down. Next letter O—okay, that one was easy. Now the letter F. That would take a whole lot of effort. I thought she was going to throw the pen at us. Next letter, again she wrote an F. We asked her, "Are you sure you mean F?" But she insisted that she knew what she wanted to say and we better pay attention. Okay, we have a "COFF," what in the world could she possibly be trying to tell us Now she was writing the letter E.

John David looked at her and said, "You want *coffee!*"

She nodded her head and continued to write. Here we go again. Can I have "S-U-G-A-R." We looked at her and said, "You want coffee with sugar." She immediately shook her head and held up fingers indicating she wanted four sugars with her coffee and also cream too.

We just laughed. This was the first time we had laughed in days. I thought to myself, *Lord, you have given this child of mine her spit-fieriness for such a time as this to show she can fight and has what it takes to overcome anything.* Now the hard part—we had to

The Window

tell her *no*! After all, how were we going to get coffee in her IV? I didn't think the nurses would allow that. I knew in that moment that my daughter was indeed going to make it. That evening her doctor came by, and he too indicated to us that he thought Stacey was going to pull through. I think he had his doubts, but then again, there is God!

Prayer: Thank you, Lord, for showing me that those who place their hope in you will not be disappointed (Isaiah 49:23). You have a perfect plan for our daughter, and you alone will fulfill that plan for her life.

CHAPTER 5

I Will Praise You Forever (Psalm 52:9).

DAY 8: It was Sunday morning, and George and I were up again and out the door, anxiously wanting to get to the hospital to see Stacey. I think we both wanted to make sure Stacey was doing as well as when we had left her the previous night. As we drove to the hospital, I thought about how far we had come over the past seven days. This whole journey with our daughter started just one week earlier, and we never dreamed all we would go through both emotionally as well as spiritually.

That morning I listened again to one of my favorite pastors on TV, and he said we as Christians grow in the midst of conflict. We will always see that God is faithful and will come through for us no matter the circumstance. He referred to Romans 8:28: "And we know that in all things God works for the good of those who love him, who have been called according to his purpose." As we drove up to the hospital, I told God, "Okay, I trust you that a lot of good is going to come out of all of this, and I know it is time for me to grow up spiritually and trust you more."

As we entered Stacey's room, she seemed even more alert. Her breathing had continued to improve with the machine doing less work in providing her with oxygen. I could tell she wanted that tube in her throat to come out, but we told her just a little longer. Being patient has never come easy for Stacey, and if we admit it, none of us likes to be patient for what we want to happen right now.

I Will Praise You Forever (Psalm 52:9).

When Stacey was nineteen, she wanted to move out and be on her own. George and I were a little shocked; we never thought she would move out until she got married. But our little Miss Independent wanted to be out of the nest and explore all that the world would offer her. She planned and prepared for her big move, but I don't think she thought it would come fast enough. She even hired movers on her own, not wanting me or George to have to do anything but help her unpack. I laugh thinking about that big day when it finally arrived and she moved all her stuff (Stacey had a lot of stuff too) into her apartment. She had a strong will as to how she wanted everything to look and where everything was to go. I must admit it, her little apartment was as cute as she was.

Stacey received a couch, end tables, and coffee table from one of her little old ladies she had done her hair for from beauty school. After Stacey had graduated from beauty school, she still continued to do some of her customers' hair. She would just go to their homes. This one little old lady just loved Stacey; she would fix her breakfast every time Stacey would come over. Stacey always had a way with older people; they just loved her.

We also contributed to her little apartment by giving her a dining room table with chairs and a little buffet to go with it. Then Stacey saved her own money and bought her first big purchase, which was her bedroom furniture. We were so proud of her for wanting to be independent.

After we had unpacked and placed everything where she wanted it to go, we got ready to say our good-byes. I noticed that Stacey seemed a little quieter at that moment, which was unusual for her. Her dad and I reached out to give her a hug, and I held back tears, not wanting to go. As we all formed a group hug, Stacey just broke down and cried. We asked her why she was crying. She said, "I worked and planned for this day; but now that it is here, I think I want to go home." We laughed, we all cried, and she stayed in her little apartment and her dad and I went home.

That seemed so long ago now as I stared at her in her bed. I kept wondering if she was going to scribble on her notepad, which she was getting pretty good

I Will Praise You Forever (Psalm 52:9).

at, for a mirror to look at herself. Thank goodness she did not. I don't think she could have stood it. I know her hair could not.

It was so nice to see some of her nurses come in who had been on different shifts and had not seen Stacey for several days. They looked so surprised when they walked into her room. I would even say they appeared to be shocked as to how well Stacey was doing, but we have a God who loves to shock and awe us. The nurses continued to adjust Stacey's machines for her to breathe more on her own. I have to admit every time they cut back on the ventilator, my heart raced a bit to see how she would respond.

As the day went by, she was now breathing at 70 percent on her own, which was great. Her doctor said he wanted to try and take her off the ventilator the next day if she continued to do well. Tomorrow couldn't come fast enough because it could be the day when I got to hear my daughter's sweet voice again.

Prayer: Lord, you have been so faithful, and your goodness is beyond anything we deserve. Thank you for being by our side every step of this journey with our daughter. It has been your presence that has sustained us and given us hope to believe. You are the God of miracles, and to you goes all the glory.

DAY 9: I don't have to tell you that I couldn't get to the hospital fast enough to witness what we believed would be a miracle. I started to think about my Bible study lesson that we were studying on this particular week, which was no coincidence. We were in John 11 where Jesus had heard that his precious friend Lazarus had died. He made the statement that this sickness would not end in death. He said it was for God's glory so that God's Son may be glorified through it. Also, he did not immediately leave where he was at to go and be with Lazarus's sisters, Mary and Martha. He waited for two days before he went to see them.

I thought about why Jesus would have waited. Again that word *wait*! Jesus could have run to Mary and Martha's side to ease their grief, yet he did not. Jesus could have easily spoken a word of healing where he was at over Lazarus and ended the grief of his loved ones, yet he did not.

I Will Praise You Forever (Psalm 52:9).

Jesus had done it before in scripture in John 4 when he healed the official's son. The royal official had sought Jesus out for him to go with him to his house and heal his son, who was close to death. Jesus just replied, "You may go. Your son will live." Just a few simple words, and this son was given restored health. While the man was on his way home, his servant met him and gave him the news that his son was living. When he asked as to the time his son got better, they told him the exact time, and it was the exact time Jesus had told him his son would live.

So why wouldn't Jesus do the same for Lazarus or that matter for my daughter? Or can I be so bold as to ask why not for all our loved ones who did not get what was hoped for in their healing? I have had many discussions with my Lord over that one. Yet there are some things in this life we will not understand, or I even think God would say this is not for us to be concerned with. What he asks us to do is to trust him and let him be who he is—and that is God—and to know we are not.

My Bible study leader once made the comment that God has the bigger picture of what we don't have or would understand. Sometimes we just have to trust him that he knows what is best. However, I know it is hard for someone who has lost a loved one. I can relate because I lost someone I loved when I was only seventeen. My father died very unexpectedly of a heart attack at only forty-six years of age.

I remember standing at his burial service watching his casket being lowered in the ground. I just stood there and asked, "*Why, God?*" Over and over I asked, "*Why?*" After what appeared to be a scene that I was creating, becoming more agitated that my question was going unanswered, I had to be led away to calm myself down. But isn't that a legitimate question that we feel God should answer? Let's be honest—why does God heal one person and not another? He loves us each equally, right? And I believe he does answer us in his Word. He tells us in John 3:16 that God so loved the world, that he gave his only begotten Son, that whosoever believeth in him should not perish, but have everlasting life. For those who know the Lord as their Savior, he promises that this earthly life won't end in death.

We will live with him eternally in heaven, and that is where we will one day unite with our loved ones who we feel have left our side way too soon.

But let us get back to Lazarus. So if Jesus knew it was God's will and plan for Lazarus to live again, why put Mary and Martha through so much pain to have to wait for this to be fulfilled? It became clear to me that the reason was simply so that God's Son may be glorified through it (John 11:4). Mary and Martha thought their situation was hopeless. After all, their brother had been dead four days. Yet they were chosen to be witnesses of the one who has power over life and death. Jesus has power over what we perceive to be hopeless situations. Can you imagine what their response was when Jesus told them to remove the stone that contained the stench of death, and then to hear Jesus tell Lazarus to come out? I bet they too leaped for joy when they witnessed their miracle and saw the glory of God.

Yes, I believed God was going to restore Stacey fully to us. I will even say there were also some days when I doubted and had to accept this may not be his will and I may have misunderstood him.

The Window

Most of all I am thankful that God fully gets us. He knows our hearts, our fears, and yes, even our doubts. Sometimes God brings us into life situations so we can know him even deeper. I can say that I had grown more spiritually with the Lord over the past few days. I had come to know him and love him in a way that I had never experienced before, and it forever changed me. As we waited for God to answer our prayers, not knowing for sure how he would answer them, he gave us his supernatural strength to go through each day just trusting him with the best outcome. His words to us each day we went up to the hospital and looked into the face of our daughter spurred us on to hope, trust, and walk in his grace.

Now the time had come. Stacey's doctor wanted to try to get her off the ventilator. This was the moment we had been praying for. If I didn't calm myself down, they were going to have to hook me up to one too. The doctor first told us of the possible complications of doing this. Why do they have to do that? But I would not let fear keep me from experiencing what I was believing God for.

I Will Praise You Forever (Psalm 52:9).

The doctor proceeded to tell us that Stacey might not be ready and they might have to keep her on the ventilator. Then there was the possibility that her vocal cords might be affected. Now that certainly wouldn't be good for Stacey, who loved to talk. He also said she would probably have to be on soft foods or liquids for a day or so. Well, she had already put pen to paper that she wanted a hamburger and fries with that cup of coffee with four sugars and cream. I certainly wouldn't be the one to tell her she couldn't have it. We were asked to leave the room to allow them to start the procedure. And where do you think I went? Straight down the hallway to the window with its sunlight bathing me in its presence. I felt the Lord's arms calming me down. I thought about Mary and Martha as they waited for their brother to come out from that tomb and be reunited with them. Now I too was waiting and praying to my God.

Prayer: God, keep my focus on you. Keep my focus on you.

The doctor and the nurses came out of Stacey's room, and I couldn't get down the hall and to her room fast enough. I noticed their faces, and they seemed to be smiling. Then I walked into her room. There was Stacey; she was off the ventilator and sitting up in her bed. Tears ran down my face as I looked at her. Yes, Lord, I had just witnessed a miracle.

Stacey started to speak. Her voice was a little strained and just a whisper, but she was talking. And rather well, I must admit. Looking at her I was so aware of God's presence. He showed us that he was in control and not Stacey's doctors. When every test came back negative and they were without answers, it was as if God said, "Not yet. When I heal this child, you will know and see it is me." When God said, "It was enough and it is my timing," then almost immediately Stacey started to improve and make a recovery. Now I was staring at her and inwardly praising God for what he had done.

I put my arms around her, able to hold her and not wanting to let go. What do you think were the first words out of her mouth? They were not, "How long have I been here?" or "What all has happened?" You got it—"Where is my cup of coffee

I Will Praise You Forever (Psalm 52:9).

and my hamburger and fries?" Well she didn't get the hamburger and fries then, but she did get her cup of coffee with four sugars and cream. Her first meal was baked chicken and mashed potatoes, and it surprised the doctors that she was able to eat that. Also she showed no signs of having any complications from being on the ventilator. It was as if Stacey went from the very brink of death to very much being alive.

As the evening went on, we got to talk and share all that had taken place over those many days. She found it very hard to believe that she had been there so long. The last thing she remembered was the day before they put her on the ventilator. We laughed at her as she thought she kept seeing the clock in her room say 2:00 in the morning and how the nurses would never leave her alone so she could get some sleep. We told her she was getting a lot of sleep since she was in a coma during those days.

And then came the question, "Where is my mirror?" Well we knew this day would come. I have to say she didn't gasp, but we got a brush to her hair and combed out every knot in it. We left shortly after the brush experience so she and John David could be alone. They needed that time to themselves. Stacey needed her husband, and her husband needed his wife; and George and I needed to go home and get a good night's sleep.

After George and I got home, we just sat awhile and talked about all God had done in getting us through these tough days. His devotional that day said in Psalm 32:8, "I will instruct you and teach you in the way you should go; I will counsel you and watch over you." That is exactly what God had been doing for us these past nine days. He did not reveal everything about his will for us and Stacey, but he did reveal everything we needed to know to trust him with the next step he was taking with us. If we had known a month earlier what we would be facing, I don't think we could have stood it. And God knew that. Therefore he didn't reveal what was around the corner, but he did prepare us with his Word so we would be strengthened when that day came. God was working in ways we didn't understand that would fortify us for this moment in time.

I Will Praise You Forever (Psalm 52:9).

Prayer: God, you know just how much we need and when we need it. You are the only one who can strengthen us for what lays ahead. Your pathway is always the best, and you will watch over us every step of the way.

Day 10: Today we were able to get Stacey out of ICU and into a regular room to complete her recovery. I was so grateful to the wonderful doctors and nurses. The care that Stacey received made me truly grateful to those who pursue the medical field, but what they do is also a gift from God that not everyone has. As I again walked down that hall to Stacey's room for the last time, I wondered how many miles I had walked down that hallway. Or for that matter, how many times had I found myself at the end of the hallway in close communion with my God at the window with its sunlight coming through. There were times when the sun was not shining, but the pull of his arms beckoned me to be near him. I would somehow miss this little window, yet I knew God was always with me. He told me over and over, "Never will I leave you, never will I forsake you" (Hebrews 13:5).

I went into Stacey's room. She was sitting up, ready and anxious to get out of ICU; if only she had realized how far she had come. There was so much I wanted to share with her, but there would be plenty of time for that. Hours seemed to drag by as we waited for the paperwork to be completed and the doctor's orders to be done. There was still one nurse I had not yet seen, and I so wanted her to see Stacey before we left. She had been such a comfort to me during those early days when we just didn't know how things would turn out.

As we both sat talking and watching TV—such a normal thing we often take for granted—I could sense Stacey wanted to say something. She went on to say, "Mama, I want to talk to you." She seemed close to tears. She told me that during the time she was on the ventilator and in a coma, she had seen people surrounding her bed. She said they kept coming and going in and out of her room. I told her that she did have lots of nurses who were constantly coming and going. She looked at me and said, "No,

I Will Praise You Forever (Psalm 52:9).

they weren't nurses. They were not like you and me; they were different. They had light all around them, and they stayed by me and surrounded me."

My heart just jumped because I knew exactly what she was talking about. I said, "Yes, honey, those indeed were God's angels that he sent to protect you. The Bible tells us in Psalm 91:11, 'For he will command his angels concerning you to guard you in all your ways.'"

I later shared with her the dream God had given me and how Jesus had told Satan he had no power here and he was not going to take our/his daughter. I wondered if Stacey had seen those angels at the exact time God had given me that dream. He was comforting both of us with his presence and his power that nothing was going to come between him and his child. Again John 10:10 comes to mind: "The thief comes only to steal and kill and destroy; I have come that they may have life, and have it to the full." I like the Amplified Bible, which states, "That they may have and enjoy life, and have it in abundance to the full, till it overflows." God was giving my daughter her life back to enjoy fully the way he intended her to have it. Again we can't stop praising God for what he has done.

During my quiet time with God, I had asked him what verse he would like me to express to those who had so diligently prayed for Stacey. I wanted it to be a verse that spoke from what my heart was feeling as well as speak of God's goodness. He was so good to give me the perfect verse in Psalm 52:9, "I will praise you forever for what you have done; in your name I will hope for your name is good. I will praise you in the presence of your saints."

Prayer: Yes, Lord, I will praise you forever for what you have done. You alone are good and deserving of all my praise.

Well the time had finally come. Every piece of paper had been signed, and we were told that they had a room upstairs waiting for Stacey. To be leaving the ICU filled me with mixed emotions. I was so thankful that we were getting out of there, yet at the same time to leave this place where Stacey got around-the-clock care by the best doctors and nurses was a little scary. I wondered if she would get

I Will Praise You Forever (Psalm 52:9).

the same care upstairs. Yet again, God reminded me, who was I trusting?

They brought a wheelchair into Stacey's room to take her upstairs. She seemed so excited to get out of that place and get on with her recovery. As we walked out of ICU, I happened to look back as if to say good-bye, and I saw the nurse I had hoped to see before we had left. I am sorry to say that I can't remember her name, but it was her compassion and kindness to me that I will never forget. I ran to her and gave her a hug. She was so glad to see Stacey doing so much better. I would even say she was a little surprised. Her smile told me she too was grateful for the outcome we had prayed for. As we wheeled Stacey out of that hallway upstairs, I was inwardly praising my God for what he had done (Psalm 52:9).

Prayer: Thank you, Lord. Your goodness to your children never ceases to amaze me. Thank you for providing the best doctors and nurses to help take care of Stacey. I trust you to keep providing her with all she needs until she walks out of this place for good.

CHAPTER 6

By Faith (Hebrews 11:1).

DAY 10, CONTINUED: As we wheeled Stacey onto the floor of her new room, it definitely seemed like we were stepping into a different atmosphere. This was indeed not ICU; there was not a sense of critical care all around us. People were coming and going, and patients were even walking themselves down the hall, looking like they were on their way to quickly going home. This would be the last stage of Stacey's journey before she would also be leaving this place. Now all she needed to do was continue to improve and regain her strength so she could be on her way to going home for good. I felt the Lord say, "Now Debra, continue to walk in faith, and believe me. I am still here with our daughter." Hebrews 11:1 says, "Now faith is being sure of what we hope for and certain of what we do not see."

Prayer: Yes, Lord, we will continue to walk in faith, for I will hold on to what I know is certain. You alone are faithful.

The Lord was indeed teaching us what walking by faith and not by sight looked like (2 Corinthians 5:7). Faith is a lot like hope. You can't see it with your eyes; it is a feeling that comes deep from within. It doesn't make sense to the unbeliever to have faith and maintain hope in something you cannot see or touch. Yet God is the one who gives us that faith to believe in him and to hope in him—to believe he is the God of the impossible and to believe he will do what he says he will do. I would even say there are times in our lives when God would ask us to step out of our comfort zone and dare to believe him to do the impossible. This is what God has asked me to do in writing this book—to step out of my

By Faith (Hebrews 11:1).

comfort zone and dare to believe him to again do the impossible for me.

Now comes the time where I feel I need to confess to how this book has even come to be written. You may tell from my writing that this journey in our daughter's life is in the past tense. In fact, this book is now several years past those difficult days that at times just seem like yesterday. If you would have told me that I would write a book about our experience, I would have told you that you were crazy. In fact, that is what I told God when he put this on my heart. It was after Stacey went home from the hospital, and I will get back to that part soon, I promise.

God came to me one afternoon as I was remembering all he had done for us and for Stacey. I was moved to tears just thinking about God's goodness and faithfulness. It was then God spoke to me to write this book. He told me the name of the book, and he laid out what each chapter was to be entitled. He even gave me the opening for the book and the closing for the book. It was the middle of the book that he was asking me to step out in faith and believe him to do the impossible one more time.

Well I would like to tell you that I immediately obeyed and told God I would trust him completely with this little endeavor he put before me, but that was not the case at all. I more or less told God he was crazy and he got the wrong person for the job. I was not about to take on doing what I thought was an impossible task.

Can you imagine that I had the nerve to question God about an impossible task after he had just done the impossible for our sweet Stacey? You know I think God at times just shakes his head at us and wonders when we are ever going to grow up. I am sure God must have felt like zapping me with a little lightning bolt from heaven, just to get my attention. But again, he was merciful to me and quickly reminded me that he had given me all the material I needed to do this *little task* for him. After all, I had been journaling the whole way through Stacey's stay at the hospital, writing down all God had done and all that we were feeling emotionally and spiritually. He even reminded me of the journal

By Faith (Hebrews 11:1).

I had started for Stacey when she was just a little girl. It was like he was saying, "I have given you all the ingredients you need. Now you just have to put them together to form a book." Oh, that sounded easy enough—*not*!

A year went by as I entertained in my mind the idea of writing this book that God had put on my heart. But every time I stepped out to begin the task, the Enemy would come along and say, "What do you think you are doing? You can't write a book; you aren't even smart enough. You don't have a college education; you don't have the skills it takes to take on such a project."

This was indeed a secret insecurity that I had, and the Enemy knew just where to stop me in my tracks. I had so many friends who had college degrees and successful careers, and I was just an ordinary mother and housewife who never finished college. As I was having my own pity party going over all my inadequacies for this job, God came to me so tenderly and said in 1 Corinthians 1:27–28, "But God chose the foolish things of the world to shame the wise; God chose the weak things of the world to shame the strong. He chose the lowly things of this world and the despised things and the things that are not to nullify the things that are."

Well that was exactly how I saw myself—weak and lowly. Okay, now that God had dismissed that excuse, I couldn't use that anymore. Then as I set out and began my writing again, feeling good about this new work that God gave me to do, once again the Enemy came to stop me in my tracks. I began thinking, *What if I am doing this out of pride?* I even contemplated that I was somehow going to take some of the glory for what God did for my daughter. Well the Enemy had taken me from feeling like an uneducated nobody to a prideful, full of myself somebody.

You know, one has to admit that Satan is very clever. I have started and stopped this book so many times, and one day God again came to me, and this time he was not as merciful as he had been the other times. He said, "How can writing this book that I asked you to do be prideful if this book is going to showcase my faithfulness to you and Stacey or even to someone who may need to read it? Either you are

By Faith (Hebrews 11:1).

going to step out in faith and believe me to enable you to write this book or you are going to disobey me and miss out on the blessings that this book is intended to give."

In that moment I had reverential fear for my Lord in what he was asking me to do. After a year of arguing with him over this book, it finally took me to a crossroad. Was I going to believe him and take the path of faith, or was I going to doubt him and take the path of disobedience? I knew this would be the last time God would ask me to step out with him and dare to believe him for what seemed impossible. I am so thankful that I chose to step out of my comfort zone and believe God to use me for whatever purpose he has for writing this book.

Well, day 10 ended very well for Stacey in her new surroundings. She got used to her new bed, not having to be attached to every machine with IV tubes going everywhere, as she had been. She looked almost like her old self too, but she still needed several days to regain her strength. She could get up out of bed now by herself and go to the bathroom, though she was a little wobbly. It is amazing how our muscles get weak after not being able to use them for days. But Stacey was determined, and it was good to see her spunk that showed everyone she was getting out of this place soon.

Stacey also started receiving visits from friends and family; they came with cards, balloons, and presents ready to spur her on to full recovery. It was so good to see Stacey visit with those precious people who had prayed so fervently for her during those tough days. I left her that evening visiting with a friend from work, and as I got into my car to leave, I started to hear that annoying little voice again say, "What if…?" What if she needed something during the night? Would the nurses be quick to react like the nurses in ICU? Maybe I should turn back around and stay the night with her just in case …

You know as mothers, we think our children will always need us, and it doesn't matter how old our children get, as mothers, we want to feel like our children still need us. Another memory comes to mind when I felt like I needed to be there for Stacey just in case she needed me. It was when she was a

By Faith (Hebrews 11:1).

teenager and was learning to drive. She had taken her driver's education course and had passed her driving test, but now she wanted to drive herself to school. I am sure those who have young teen drivers can relate to this one. You panic thinking, *Will they pay attention? Will they be quick enough to react to a dangerous situation? Will they obey the speed limit?* The list goes on.

She had proven herself to be a good driver, and her school was only a couple of miles down the road, but I still just didn't feel like she was ready. Truth be told, I was the one who was not quite ready to let my child loose on the road in a car.

Well I came up with what I thought was a good solution for her to be able to drive to school and for me, the overprotective mother, to let her drive to school alone—well, somewhat alone. I told her that she could drive, but I was going to follow her in my car as she drove to school, and I would be there promptly when school got out to follow her back home. Well you can visualize the look I received, but she accepted my proposal; at least she got to drive.

Can you imagine how embarrassing this must have been for her? But Stacey never once complained to me. So every morning off to school we went. It was Stacey the ever-so-careful driver and her overprotective mother following right behind her, ready to bounce on anyone who dared to run into her or worse, try and cut her off on the road. Super-Mother would be there to protect her young. Then every afternoon I was in that parking lot right behind her parked car waiting for her to get out of class. Stacey must have wished she had on some disguise so no one would recognize that it was her paranoid mother waiting to follow her home.

Oh how I laughed. I am sure she wanted to kill me, especially when I waved to everyone who walked by just to let them know it was indeed Stacey's mother. That was our little routine for about a month, until I felt like I could let her drive by herself. Well truth be told, I think she took up her cause with her dad, who told his wife it was time to back off and let her drive herself to school.

This was again where I needed to step out in faith and trust the nurses to do their jobs and most

By Faith (Hebrews 11:1).

of all trust God to be faithful to do what he said he would do.

Prayer: Thank you, Lord, for being who you are. You alone are faithful and good. You alone are trustworthy to do all that you said you would do. Thank you also, Lord, for being so patient with me and not treating me as my sins deserve. Thank you for teaching me and helping me to walk by faith and not by sight.

DAY 11: I didn't rush to get to the hospital as quick as I had all those other days. I think I even sat and had an extra cup of coffee. After ten days of getting little sleep and rushing to the hospital every morning early, I could now relax and let friends and family go and spend time with Stacey. While I was running a few errands before going up to the hospital, I thought it might be a good idea for Stacey to write thank you cards to everyone at the hospital who had been so wonderful to her. She had so many amazing nurses and doctors who truly cared for her, and I thought this could be a way for her to show her gratitude. As for my part, I planned on making my (oh-so-good) brownies for everyone.

When I got to Stacey's room ready to show her these cards I bought, I saw a worried look on her face. She was sitting up in her bed, and she had a rash all over her chest. The doctors and nurses didn't seem concerned, but Stacey was anxious. I think the enormity of everything she had gone through was starting to set in. I could feel that this was one last jab the Enemy was using to get us rattled. God was quick to refocus me and again give us his word in Job 42:2, "I know that you can do all things; no plan of yours can be thwarted" and Deuteronomy 32:46, "Take to heart all the words I have solemnly declared to you this day."

Standing firm on God's promises is not always easy, especially when Satan tries to throw us off track. Sometimes we take several steps forward, feeling strong and confident, but then something happens and we take a few steps back. But what is so awesome about God is his promises are firm. We may at times feel weak, but our God is strong.

By Faith (Hebrews 11:1).

When Stacey was ten months old, you could tell she was going to start walking early. She would hold onto things and try to walk around them. Even at a young age, she was determined to do what she wanted to do, and that was to walk on her own. As we were celebrating Thanksgiving that year with family, we placed her playpen next to the dining room so we could watch her as we ate. I would glance over at her as she held onto the playpen and walked around it. You could tell she was getting pretty confident as she quickly circled that playpen several times, and then all of a sudden the desire to get to where she wanted to go was more important than the fear of falling. She reached out her hand toward the other side of the playpen and let go of the other hand, which was holding on. She took a step, then another step, and before I could say a word to everyone around the table, she was across the playpen with a big grin on her face. We clapped our hands at her accomplishment; she was such a big girl.

Sometimes I think God too applauds us when we let go of fear and trust him with our faith. He

The Window

spurs us on to each step of believing him, trusting him, and leaving that fear of whatever behind us.

Stacey seemed a little more at peace as the day went on. It helped that more friends and family came to see her. She would talk and laugh with them and make plans of very soon getting out of that place. I too was making plans that went beyond the hospital, though I was so grateful for it. It was good to think of just having a normal routine again.

Prayer: Lord, thank you for being who you are: faithful and good. Your path for us may not always be an easy one, and it may not be even a path we would choose for ourselves. But it helps knowing you are ahead of us in ways we cannot see or know making that path smooth for us to follow you.

CHAPTER 7

Those Who Hope in Me Will Not Be Disappointed (Isaiah 49:23).

DAY 12: As I walked into Stacey's room that morning, she was sitting in her bed working on her thank-you cards. I truly think this was a blessing because it kept her mind occupied and off of the boredom she was starting to feel. Her rash was looking a little better, and her doctors were saying she could go home tomorrow.

The Window

Well that day could not come fast enough for Stacey. She was ready to get out of that place and get on with her life. She wanted to return to work as soon as possible and show everyone that she was truly back among the living. Her job consisted of her being on the phone a lot, so it was good that her voice was now back to normal. Also, her bosses at work were very understanding of Stacey's health crisis because John David had been in constant contact with them to give updates on Stacey's progress.

Stacey's doctors, however, gave some strict restrictions regarding her job. She could only start off with working half days to see how her strength progressed. She would also have to see one of her doctors who had been with her since the very beginning. This was her lung doctor, the one who wanted to beat his head against the wall, saying, "This is really kicking my butt." We had come to really appreciate his deep concern for Stacey, and I believe he had really become attached to this little patient of his. Stacey would also have to follow up

Those Who Hope in Me Will Not Be Disappointed (Isaiah 49:23).

with the urologist to make sure there were no lasting effects from the complications she had.

But overall, all we heard was she could go home tomorrow, and tomorrow couldn't come fast enough. As we walked around her floor, which she was starting to do without getting too tired and out of breath, we planned on how we would say our good-byes to everyone and hand out her thank-you notes and my oh-so-good brownies to those who had meant so much to us. Tomorrow would be a good day—a day of praising God for what he had done. It would be day of remembering that those who hope in him will not be disappointed (Isaiah 49:23).

Saying good-byes can sometimes be hard, especially if it is to a friend we love dearly or to a place like a home we have lived in for years. But saying good-bye opens the door for what lays ahead—to a future filled with life's blessings that God has gone before and prepared for us. His Word even says in 1 Corinthians 2:9, "No eye has seen, no ear has heard, no mind has conceived what God has prepared for those who love him."

The Window

Several years ago God gave me a life lesson on what good-byes can look like. We had a family of doves that had made their nest in one of our trees in our backyard. I loved watching those doves take care of their little babies. One parent was always with the nest as the other one went and got food. Every day I would go out and talk to those little birds, telling them how big they were getting. The mama dove must have sensed that I too was a mama and she could somehow trust me in close proximity to her young.

Well, soon it became time for those little birds to learn how to fly in order to leave the nest they had come to love and felt protected in. But there was one little dove that had no intentions of learning how to fly. I think he liked everything just the way it was. I would go out there and talk to him, telling him he could do it—he could fly and leave his nest behind. I would often see the mama dove on the backyard fence as she watched her little bird all alone. Several days went by, and this little bird was still hanging onto his home. He would venture out just a little to a branch that was close to the nest, as

Those Who Hope in Me Will Not Be Disappointed (Isaiah 49:23).

if he was trying to get up the courage to fly. I would go out and tell him he could do it; he was a big bird, he could fly. My family laughed at me talking to these little birds, but I thought even God's littlest creations could use some encouragement too.

One day as I was preparing to leave for my Bible study, I went out to see if this little bird was still hanging around and there he was. He had ventured out farther onto a branch that was closest to the ground. I gave him one last pep talk and went on my way, wondering if he would still be there when I returned. As soon as I got home, I went to see if he had gotten enough courage to finally fly away and say good-bye to his home, and he had. Over the next few days I would look out in the backyard, and I would see this little dove perched on the fence looking into the yard, as if to let me know he had learned to fly and he was doing just fine. At least that is what I think he was saying; I don't want it out that I talk to the birds at least not on a regular basis.

Now God was preparing Stacey to say good-bye to this chapter in her life and trust him to go before her to a life filled with hopes and dreams that he had prepared just for her. As for me, saying goodbye would not be hard because I was ready to see Stacey leave this place. What I was going to miss the most was that little window in ICU where God and I met on a regular basis. It was at that window that I experienced the love of God that helped me to release my fears into his hands, trusting him with one of my most precious gifts, my little girl. I will carry those memories with me all the days of my life, and I will forever thank him for what he has done.

I left Stacey that evening, eager and excited for tomorrow to come. She was not going to be like that little dove in our backyard all those years ago; she was ready to fly out of this place to a new beginning. Tomorrow was what we had been praying for; tomorrow would be a day of rejoicing.

Prayer: Lord, you alone have been with us on this entire journey with our daughter. Never did you once leave our side. You have been faithful; you have been good. My heart is overflowing with your love.

Those Who Hope in Me Will Not Be Disappointed (Isaiah 49:23).

DAY 13: I don't have to tell you how eager I was to get to the hospital, which would be the last time. I was eager to see this chapter in our daughter's life come to an end. But you can't move forward without knowing and understanding where you have been. For us looking back was seeing the faithfulness of our God, and looking forward was also seeing the faithfulness of God to take us on a new path with him showing us the way.

As I walked down the hallway to Stacey's room, I had several batches of my oh-so-good brownies with me, ready to give out to the doctors and nurses who had been such a blessing to us. As I entered Stacey's room, there she was all dressed and ready to escape this place. John David had brought her some clothes from home, along with her makeup and all her hair products. Oh her hair looked so much better than those days when it looked like a bird's nest piled on top of her head. No longer did she look like the patient. She beamed with new health, restored health from our God.

I think her first words as I walked into the room were, "When can I leave?" Well there were, of course, all the paperwork and discharge papers that had to be signed. It was just like it was when we left ICU to come to this new floor every "I" had to be dotted and every "T" had to be crossed. There were also plenty of instructions for going home that Stacey had to swear she would follow.

As we waited for all of this to be done, we set out into the hospital with thank-you cards and brownies in tow. Knowing we had a lot of places and people to see, Stacey rode in her wheelchair while her mother became her driver. I laugh thinking how silly we must have looked. I am sure you could hear us coming as we laughed and I whizzed Stacey around in her wheelchair. I was surprised we weren't pulled over and given a warning for too much laughter and too much fun.

As we passed out our goodies to the staff on her floor, we were met with cheers and good health from all the nurses. We then made our way to the pulmonary department, where Stacey had received excellent care from the nurses and technicians that helped her regain strength in her lungs. There too we were met with smiles and thank-yous. It seemed,

Those Who Hope in Me Will Not Be Disappointed (Isaiah 49:23).

though, that the staff was not used to receiving such warm and heartfelt appreciation from their patients. But what we were handing out to them was only a small gesture of what our hearts truly felt.

Now we had only one more place to go, and that was to ICU. This was the place I would always remember and be forever grateful for their expert care and concern for Stacey. As we wheeled into the ICU, I could sense everyone's eyes turning to greet us. Instantly there were smiles on their faces as they approached their once-so-sick little patient. There were many who came whose faces I didn't remember, but I think they too must have heard about this little patient who experienced a miracle. Stacey and I expressed our appreciation to each one as we gave them their thank-you cards and brownies. You could tell that this meant a lot, something they too were not used to receiving. It felt good to come by one last time and say good-bye and to let them see how improved their patient had become. As we approached the doors to leave, I looked back once more to glance at that little window at the end of

The Window

the hallway, and with a smile on my face, I inwardly said good-bye and praised my God.

Prayer: Lord, you are the one who we praise in restoring our daughter's health. You are the reason our joy overflows.

The time had finally come. We were back in Stacey's room, and her walking papers were waiting for her to sign. We gathered all her belongings that she had accumulated during the past thirteen days. We had flowers, balloons, and even a little teddy bear that a dear friend from church had given Stacey. As John David got the car to pick up his beloved wife, I noticed that it had started to rain. It wasn't a hard rain but just enough that made me think that our Lord was making it rain to wash all the pollutants from the air so it would be clean and fresh as Stacey stepped out of the hospital to take her first breath of fresh air in thirteen days.

How good of God to even care that his child should have fresh air to breathe as she left the past behind her and breathed deeply for what lay ahead. With that he reminded me again that he was with my Stacey. His Word in Psalm 121:7–8 says, "He

Those Who Hope in Me Will Not Be Disappointed (Isaiah 49:23).

will watch over your life, the Lord will watch over your coming and going both now and forevermore." Well, Stacey walked out of those doors and took her first breath of fresh air while bundled up because it was still cold outside. John David put his wife in their car, and as they drove off, I said, "Praise God. In the midst of pain, I have seen your glory. In the midst of pain, Lord, you are there. It is your tender loving mercies that have wiped away these mother's tears."

PERSONAL NOTE FROM DEBRA

As I say good-bye to this chapter in our family's life, I want to openly express my gratitude to my Lord and Savior for his faithfulness to me in completing this book. I will forever be grateful to my Lord for not giving up on me when at times I wanted to give up on myself. This book was written to showcase God's faithfulness to our family. I may never know this side of heaven what God has in store for this book, and that is okay. What matters is God has a plan, and what he asked of me was to trust him with the outcome. So I lay down this book as a sacrifice of praise to my Lord for what he has done.

And to the person who may one day read this book and question where God is in your situation, please know he is never far from those who call on him (Psalm 145:18). Sometimes, though, he allows us to come to the end of ourselves so we can understand that we can't do things on our own. We need a Savior who has gone before us, and that Savior is Jesus Christ himself. You cannot truly know what faith in God means or know what having hope in him is without first experiencing the love of God that comes from believing in his Son Jesus Christ.

Jesus himself answered his disciples in John 14:6, "I am the way and the truth and the life, No one comes to the Father except through me." To know Jesus as your Savior is to first acknowledge that you need a Savior. God sent Jesus to this world to save us from our sins (John 3:16). It is our sins that separate us from God (Romans 3:23).

If this book has caused you to sense that something is missing in your life, then maybe God is trying to show you that something is his Son, Jesus Christ. Simply acknowledge that you are a sinner and need the forgiveness that only Jesus can give (Ephesians 1:7). He never turns those away who seek him in truth. Believe him now to be the one who died for your sins and lives today in heaven, seated at the right hand of God, interceding for you with the Father (Hebrews 7:25). Accept him and receive him now as your Lord and Savior. His love never fails, and you can trust him with whatever comes into your life today. And because we have experienced that love, we too can trust him with whatever else comes in our lives.

Prayer: Dear Father, may those who don't know you as Lord come to know you as their Savior so they can experience for themselves the wonder of your love and the wonder of your faithfulness. And to those who know you as I do but need just a little reassurance of your love, may your arms embrace them now and come quickly to help them in their circumstance. In Jesus' name I pray, amen.

SHARED MEMORIES

1-Stacey learning to walk with her mother's help

2-Stacey doing her best MC Hammer impersonation

3-Stacey as a Zavala Lion cheerleader

4-Stacey and George going to a
Daddy / Daughter Banquet

5-Stacey in 7th grade at Dallas Baptist University Lab School

6-Stacey winning third place at National Skating competition in California

7-Stacey and John David on their wedding day

8-Stacey with Allegra and Marissa

9-Family photo at wedding reception

10-Daddy / Daughter dance at wedding reception

11-Stacey and Debra today

Printed in the United States
By Bookmasters